CW01333836

TRIUMPH HOUSE
Poetry with a Purpose

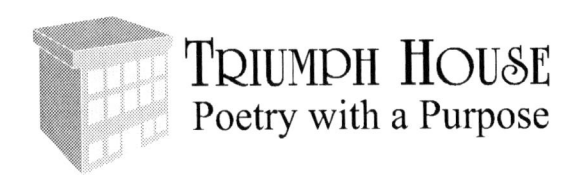

SOUL REFLECTION

Edited by

Steve Twelvetree

First published in Great Britain in 1999 by
TRIUMPH HOUSE
Remus House,
Coltsfoot Drive,
Woodston,
Peterborough, PE2 9JX
Telephone (01733) 898102

All Rights Reserved

Copyright Contributors 1999

HB ISBN 1 86161 554 X
SB ISBN 1 86161 559 0

CONTENTS

Please God	Richard Reeve	1
God, My Friend	Wilma West	2
Bedtime	Lucy Price	3
While We're Sleeping	Claire Farragher	4
Healing Rainbow	Sara Newby	5
Talking To Jesus	Janet Hewitt	6
Till We Meet Again	Margaret Jean Medlock	7
The Shepherd	Nick Purchase	8
Eventide	Ray Lennard	9
Keep Us Safe . . .	Marilyn M Fowler	10
It's Time . . .	Hannah Bunclark	11
Bedtime Thoughts	Ann Rutherford	12
My Pretty One	Gig	13
Resting Place	Belinda J Howells	14
Night Comes	Anne MacLeod	15
Always	William Lowe	16
A Bedtime Poem	Phyllis M Dunn	17
Bedtime Prayer	Joan Heybourn	18
Evening Thoughts	Hazel Cooper	19
Surrender	Elizabeth Wynne	20
Dreamtime	Sheila Waller	21
Pray	Anne McTavish	22
A Tired Wish	C Halliburton	23
My Prayer	Tina Smith	24
Thoughts Of A Child	Terry Coneys	25
Peace	Maureen Henderson	26
Only A Whisper Away	Lilian Cherry	27
Since I Am Yours	Dorinda MacDowell	28
Voyage To Eternity	Jennie Fletcher	29
Restful Sleep	Carole Revell	30
My Guiding Light	S Bishop	31
A Prayer For My Love	Ann Duncan	32
Thoughts	June Christensen	33
Silence	Rita Hillier	34
Loving Prayer	Christine Shurey	35
Prayer Of A Dancer	Mary McCaig	36

The Meditators	Jean Paisley	37
Experience	Iris Cone	38
Bedtime Prayer	B Bowles	39
Peace Within	Maud Sales	40
Heavenly Bliss	John de Graft-Hayford	41
I Give Thanks	Barbara O'Grady	42
Hope In Your Heart	Erica Gordon	43
Prayer And Peace	Pat Melbourn	44
Prayer Of Love	Anita Messer	45
The Sleep Fairies	Daren Peary	46
Lullaby	Benny Howell	47
You Are There	Maureen Bell	48
Give Me Strength	Jean Oxley	49
Child's Prayer	Elaine Sturman	50
A Prayer For Anyone	Jacquie Richardson	51
A Prayer For Fulfilment	Carole Fowles	52
God Sent Us	Alien 3	53
Positive	N C Bain	54
The Ageing Night	Shirley Sammout	55
Child	Helen Mary Miller	56
I Thank You	Joleen McPartland	57
The Bogeyman	Carol McCann	58
A Prayer For Tonight	S Askew	60
A Child's Prayer	Dawn Parsons	61
Sailing Sleepy Seas	C MacAlister-Cottrill	62
My Prayer	Pauline Conlon	63
Be Near Us Lord	J Winwood	64
Heavenly Tranquillity	Kelly Hurn	65
Prayer For The Start Of Each Day And Night	P Pattel	66
A 'Curative' Prayer	Robert Hessey	67
Thoughts Of Mine Own	Denys George Hill	68
Abbey Dear	Abbey	69
Gratitude	Deborah Hall	70
Souls	Joan M Tapping	71
Bedtime Dreamtime	Sarah L Scotcher	72
A New Day Will Dawn	Valerie M Bacon	73
The World Of Sleep	John Hooley	74

Lord How Long?	Maggie Roberts	75
A Single Rose	Philip London	76
A Prayer For Everyone	Grace D Frackleton	77
My Prayer	J Painting	78
The Strife Of Life?	John P Evans	79
Thank You	K Lake	80
Parental Poetry	Teresa Webb	81
Not Just A Bedtime Prayer	Frances Doe	82
A Goodnight Kiss	Philip Trivett	83
Untitled	Yvonne Johnson	84
Evening Prayer	Sheila St Clair	85
It Was One Of Those Days, Lord!	J V Lisle	86
When You Sleep	Katie Burt	87
Thank You	Susan Davies	88
The Panda	Evelyn Sharman	89
A Child's Prayer	Geo K Phillips	90
A Bedtime Prayer	Tracey Marie	91
Bless You All	Sheila Wall	92
Song For A Full Moon	Laura Cruickshank	93
Guidance	N Callear	94
Poem For A Child	Ann Grimwood	95
The Last Prayer	John Amsden	96
Private Conference	Jacqueline Lopez	97
A Cry In The Wilderness	George Lockwood	98
The Pole Star	Irene Gunnion	99
Into God's Hands	Anne Sanderson	100
Catch The Sunshine	Ann Hathaway	101

PLEASE GOD

Please God, I always say,
Send my Giro tomorrow,
The children need, they always do,
New shoes and then there is the baby,
That's if my Giro comes.

Please God, I always say,
Don't let it rain tomorrow,
Young John, that's my eldest one,
Has got to have a Mac,
That's if my Giro comes.

Please God, I always say,
It's rent again tomorrow
So help me pay this week,
What do I do about it all,
Please God, I say, help me.

Richard Reeve

GOD, MY FRIEND

At times the pain and grief
Threaten to overwhelm me
The anguish and torment
Threaten to consume me
At times like these
God is my only friend
I pray for help
I pray for courage
I pray for strength
And I pray for release
From my personal prison.
Today dear Lord
Give me peace
Thank you Father
For being my friend.

Wilma West

FOREWORD

Many people across the world give praise and thanks each night using either 'The Lord's Prayer' or even a special prayer of their own. Often these prayers pay homage to the great things we have and will also ask for the well-being of family, friends and people in need.

Soul Reflection is a unique collection of these thoughts, feelings and thanks, carefully harvested and selected for your own reading pleasure.

Each talented author within shares a message from both the heart and soul offering true inspiration for those in need. The result is a timely collection of poems and prayers sure to delight for many years to come.

Steve Twelvetree
Editor

BEDTIME

As you climb into chimerical night clothes,
You gaze out on to luminary stars,
Glowing bright and white and yellow
Through the taciturn twilight
Into your wishy-washy windows.

In the distance the moon swirls in a sluggish satellite
Orbiting your reflected reveries,
Transporting you into a torpid trance.

The teddy-bear snuggles down beneath the blanket,
Coverlets of musing melodies,
Lullabies of lethargic litanies
Creep up through the darkness,
Concealing cryptic messages
Which ooze through the enigmatic nightfall.

Sleep comes easy,
Now the bedbugs bite the dusk.

Lucy Price

WHILE WE'RE SLEEPING

All I ask of you is to keep me wrapped up warm
To make me feel protected from the world
All I ask of you is to keep me dry from the storm
To keep me safe in this bed.

And all I ever ask of you
Is that while I'm sleeping
Dear God keep me breathing
All I ever ask of you is to keep my people safe
To let them sleep so undisturbed
To let them sleep without being heard
By the devils of the night
Dear God tell me they'll be alright.

All I ask of you is to keep my soul rested
To relax my body and mind
All I ask of you is to tuck me up in bed
Dear God keep me safe and sound.

And all I'll ever, ever ask of you
Is that while I'm sleeping
Dear God please keep me breathing
And all I'll ever ask of you
Is that while they're sleeping
Dear God please keep them breathing.

Claire Farragher

HEALING RAINBOW

I'm sending you red for energy
And orange to see you through.
Yellow to bring you sunshine
For tranquillity, green and blue
Violet for the daytime sky
And Indigo for the night
This is your rainbow cloak
To wrap around you tight.
I'm sending you all my prayers
And my love and healing too
So whenever you see a rainbow
God made it just for you

Sara Newby

TALKING TO JESUS

Jesus, I'm ready to repose.
As my heavy eyelids close,
May my thoughts be of you
Bless me this night through.

Protect my friends, family,
A Guardian Angel be with me.
May dreams not spoil my rest.
My Lord, this is my request.

Every wrong I've done today,
Or said, even thought, I pray,
That You'll forgive me please,
So my mind will be at ease.

When I wake up, Lord, I ask,
For energy to fulfil each task;
My sleep having been enough,
That they won't be too tough.

And thank You for Your love,
Knowing it will leave me never;
That one day in Heaven above,
I will dwell with You forever.

Amen.

Janet Hewitt

TILL WE MEET AGAIN

As I lay my head on my pillow,
your body next to mine,
tears of sorrow fill my eyes,
for I know we have little time
I feel your arms around me,
Your gentle breath on my face,
through midst of tears I touch you ,
and feel your warm embrace.
I know you are going to leave me,
and I prayed you wouldn't go alone.
I asked the good Lord to guide you,
when he silently called you home.
But not today, I begged him,
please give us a little more time,
but today it had to be,
you were, no longer mine.
So walk with the angels, my darling,
far away in the garden of rest.
Kiss away my tears as I'm sleeping,
for here on earth you were one of the best.

Margaret Jean Medlock

THE SHEPHERD

Be not afraid in life sublime
Use hope as wings and merrily climb.
When the will of flesh is weak
My voice in spirit shall speak,
There is nothing that is yours but Mine.

I am the flame of suns so bright
I am the shepherd of starry night;
I am the guest and host
The watcher at the post,
I am your love and you are My light.

If you but give yourself to Me
Not in doubt but whole heartily;
Your open prayers I shall heed
When you call to Me in need,
You are a wave and I the endless sea.

All things come true if you believe.

Nick Purchase

EVENTIDE

Now eventide as I pray
Thank you Lord for joys each day,
Each day we live, give our best
Until we take eternal rest.

Ray Lennard

KEEP US SAFE...

Gentle Jesus in the sky above
Look upon the ones you love,
Keep us safe throughout each day,
Teach us to be good and pray.
Take away our pains and sorrow
Pray, let our worries ease tomorrow.
Keep us safe throughout this night
And bear with us 'til morning light.

Amen

Marilyn M Fowler

IT'S TIME...

It's time to close my sleepy eyes,
And lay me down to rest,
That when I wake, I pray my Lord,
I'll strive to do my best.

Hannah Bunclark

BEDTIME THOUGHTS

As I prepare for bed at night
keep me in Your care,
and hear my grateful thanks, O God,
in this simple prayer.

For all the blessings of the day,
for family and friends,
for safety as the night draws near
as the daylight ends.

And when the night has passed away
and sunshine paints the dawn
please God wake me in grateful mood
to greet the coming morn.

Ann Rutherford

MY PRETTY ONE

Close your eyes, pretty one
Soon the darkness be gone
You shall wake to a brand-new day
Dream your dreams, pretty one
When the morning does come
Then with friends, you may go out and play
You can laugh, sing, and do anything
But for now, close your eyes, my pretty one.

Say your prayers, my pretty one
Thank the lord, the day is done
To keep us safe, till next morning light
For the food that we eat
The blessing of sleep
And the stars, that shine every night
You will be good, as you should
And thank him more if you could
But for now, close your eyes, my pretty one . . .

Gig

RESTING PLACE

Thank you Lord
As I settle to sleep
Let me rest peacefully
As your love enfolds me
I lie in your arms
The wings of shelter
Which encompass me
Thank you for your love
And your shelter
The life you breathe in me
That my spirit and yours are entwined
As I come to rest, I momentarily
Think of the eagle
Soaring high above your Earth
High above the element, high into the sky
As he flies on the edge of the wind
But then he comes to rest
He returns to his eyrie
To reassess and to rest
As I am coming to rest
To sleep with the knowledge
That with you, tomorrow
I shall soar, I shall fly
But for now I rest in
The shadow of your wings
In the presence of peace
Thank you Lord.

Belinda J Howells

NIGHT COMES

I sit
I wait my love
for you out there.
I am alone
who is there to care?

Twilight descends.
I think.
My dreams chase round.
I listen for the sound
of you out there.

Dark has come.
I lie.
The spirit within
has broken free
to be with thee.

Anne MacLeod

ALWAYS

Each night before I go to sleep
I send you all my love, my sweet.
I open my palm and blow a kiss
Then close my eyes and make a wish.
I wish that you were by my side
And that one day you'll be my bride.
Although I lie alone at night
I feel your presence holding me tight
And when I awaken from my sleep
I know our love is always for keeps.

William Lowe

A BEDTIME POEM

Nightly before I lie on my bed
I kneel on the floor to pray.
My day has been good
but I know that I should
think of others so far away.
Tired, hungry and cold
the young and the old.
Far from home, some alone.
Lord in thy mercy,
Hear my prayer,
Amen.

Phyllis M Dunn

BEDTIME PRAYER

Father God, the night is dark
And pain seems hard to bear
As I kneel before You now
Please hear my bedtime prayer.

Jesus, Lord, please grant me rest
As moonlight shadows creep
The nightime hours seem longest
When it's difficult to sleep . . .

Send Your Holy Spirit Lord
And guardian angels, too,
May this be asking little,
For I put my trust in You.

Lord, in Your heavenly mansions
Where there is no more pain
The cares of Earth will vanish
All will be new again.

Lord, be with me all night through
Please let me feel Your peace
Till morning skies herald dawn
And daylight hours increase.

Then during the coming day
Remain close by my side,
I need Thee every hour
To be my Friend and Guide.

Lord I give this prayer to You
I know You understand,
Thank You for every blessing
From Your Almighty hand.

Joan Heybourn

EVENING THOUGHTS

O Lord, we thank You for the beauty of each day
Thank You for new growth in the spring
Summer heat and flowering shrubs
Winter cold, snow and icy beauty on trees and bushes.
Help us to appreciate all of your goodness and the
                                               wonders of this world.
For those whose day has been filled with sadness
Those who are in pain or suffering in any way,
Please be with them all.
Comfort those who mourn
Give those who care for the sick and handicapped the
                                            strength to carry on each day.
Help us to forget ourselves and think of others
Put your loving arms around them all.
Be with children in hospital and the nurses and doctors who
                                               minister to them
Grant we pray forgiveness for unloving thoughts and deeds
For not speaking when we should and saying things we shouldn't say
Now in the evening as the light disappears and shadows lengthen
Give us the calmness of spirit as we go to bed
Safe in the knowledge that you are with us
Hand in hand with each other and Thee.

Hazel Cooper

SURRENDER

Letting go and letting God.
Resting in the everlasting arms.
Glib words, or comforting strength,
What is the depth of our receiving?
Do we sleep in perfect peace,
Tranquil, balanced and in harmony?
Can our bedtime be calm deep breathing,
Floating free of the world's deceiving?
Ask and it is given.
Trusting in that space called Heaven.

Elizabeth Wynne

DREAMTIME

Time to rest your sleepy head
Tucked up warm in your cosy bed
Sleep peacefully on a cloud of dreams
Under the glow of soft moonbeams.
May you rest in peace this night
Free from pain until morning light
Embraced by thoughts by ones you love
Blessed by angels way up above
Until sun rises in early dawn
Begin again a fresh new dawn.

Sheila Waller

PRAY

I pray to the Lord to guide me,
through each living day.
I pray to the Lord to help me,
in each mistake I make.
But in my heart I know
the Lord loves me,
with each daybreak.

Anne McTavish

A Tired Wish

Lord I rest my weary eyes
As I look up to the darkened skies
I wish up upon a twinkling star
Hoping you are with us wherever
we are.

C Halliburton

MY PRAYER

When I go to bed at night,
I pray the world will be alright
That people in the far off lands,
Will live as one, as God commands.

Whilst in their search for perfect peace,
Their hurt and suffering soon will cease.
Then perfect is the human race,
Where man and beast will take their place.

We watch the sun rise in the sky,
Observe the world through psychic eye.
And every night I hope and pray,
This earth will see another day.

With guidance from our God above,
The Universe is filled with love.
We look in wonder at the sight,
Of his creation, and his might.

Please guide me as I walk along,
This precious path I tread upon.
If it looks like I might stray,
Help me find the Christian way.

As I close my eyes so tight,
God bless everyone this night.
Grant them wishes; heal their sorrow,
I'll pray for them again tomorrow.

Tina Smith

THOUGHTS OF A CHILD

Why's the sky so blue and high?
Who makes the clouds? Who sends the breeze?
Why is it that birds can fly?
Is the moon made up of cheese?

Why's Christmas only once a year?
Why not every day?
I'm sure that Santa wouldn't mind coming on his sleigh.

Is it true that robins playing in the sun,
Get their breasts all sunburned
While having lots of fun?

Is it true when God is angry he makes the thunder sound?
And is there really an old Jack Frost where icicles are found?

What makes the snow so bright and white?
And where do snowmen go?
What turns daylight into night?
Who makes the stars all glow?

Can you walk along a rainbow and jump off at the end?
Who paints all the colours on it right across the bend?
Is there really a guardian angel looking after me?
Is it true that God has sent her and I'm not allowed to see?

And when I say my prayers at night,
Then into bed I creep.
I'm always asking God for answers,
But I always fall asleep.

Terry Coneys

PEACE

At the close of another day
For my family and friends I hope and pray
To bring them peace from above
That they feel the joy of being loved

That they should know for them I pray
That we are able to greet a brand-new day
To wish them all peace of mind
The greatest gift to all mankind.

Maureen Henderson

ONLY A WHISPER AWAY

The songbirds are singing in the trees,
to the gentle sighing of the breeze.
I look around me, but you're not here,
only the shadows in the evening air.
Then you come to me in a moment of grace,
with that same smile upon your face.
'Tis then I hear you softly say,
'Don't worry, I'm only a whisper away.'

Lilian Cherry

SINCE I AM YOURS

Since I am Yours
And You are mine
Let my whole being
Be wholly Thine . . .

Yes, outwardly -
For all to see
How Jesus' love
Enraptures me . . .

But, more, within -
Yes, even to
My soul; its life
Belongs to You . . .

So take my thoughts -
From whence each deed
Springs into life -
For, Lord, I need

Your guidance so,
For I am weak
And strong are You -
That strength I seek . . .

So take my thoughts,
Control them, Lord,
Till they meet Yours
In sweet accord.

Dorinda MacDowell

VOYAGE TO ETERNITY

I am captain of my soul,
Alongside my chosen crew,
I am on an unknown course,
Which you alone can bring me through.
You are my rainbow amid life's storms,
My anchor in life's sea.
I ask for understanding and guidance in my frailty.
Dear Lord I pray tonight,
Enlighten me.

Jennie Fletcher

RESTFUL SLEEP

Let me rest in the peace of slumber,
Keep my soul safe throughout this night.
Walk with me in the field of dreams.
Enfold me within your light.

Help keep away the nightmares,
Watch by my bed until dawn,
And with the sun let me rise again
To face the bright new morn.

I know not what the day may bring,
But Your grace will see me through,
For I walk the path Your Son once trod.
All my pain is known by You.

When I stumble on life's pathway,
Help me to be aware
Of hands reaching out to help me
With tender loving care.

So let me rest for a while in tranquillity,
Heal the body, spirit and mind.
Give me strength to face tomorrow
Knowing you walk but a step behind.

Carole Revell

MY GUIDING LIGHT

Lord I pray to thee above
Give us your eternal love.
Keep us safe by day and night
Surrounded by your heavenly light.
In your loving arms enfold
All of us both young and old.
Give us strength throughout the day
Help us Lord to carry on.
Give us guidance from above
To help and comfort those we love.
Show all people far and wide
That you are walking by their side.
When days seem long and hard to bear
Reach out to show us that you care.

S Bishop

A Prayer For My Love

When I die
And leave you here,
Know that my soul
Lives on,
In a new dimension,
Invisible, untouchable,
Waiting for the moment
When once more united,
We fly away
Into forever.

Until that day,
Holding my memory
In a far corner
Of your heart,
Live your life to the brim.
Though my spirit
Will depart,
And my body
Will moulder to ashes,
My love will live on.

When pain and loneliness
Empty your world,
Just breathe my name
In your heart.
Wherever I am,
My spirit will hear
And I will come to you.
I will comfort you,
I will be there.
I *will* be there.

Ann Duncan

THOUGHTS

I say my prayers every night
For all the wrongs to be put right.
I pray for husband, son and daughter
To join together if one should falter.

A special prayer for Wade and Neil
To grow up strong, kind and not to steal.
A silent prayer for all my friends
Remember this is not the end.

June Christensen

Silence

In the silence,
of the moment,
in the silence,
of the hour,
may I find within it
all Your awesome power.
Only You Lord
can change within me,
thoughts
that should not be.
Only You, Lord,
make the changes,
in the world,
also in me.
So in the silence,
of the moment,
may I feel,
Your wondrous calm.
Knowing Lord,
that You love me
and no one
can do me harm.

Rita Hillier

LOVING PRAYER

O mighty Lord Jesus I come to thee,
I lay my head upon your breast.
O loving Saviour your child will give you praise
for my food and lovely warm bed, safe from harm.
Loving Saviour I come to thee,
I give you all my heart and soul to keep forever and ever.
Never leave me alone.
Hallelujah Blessed Jesus be in my mouth,
that I may speak with a warm heart,
loving words to soothe sorrowful hearts.
Peace be still in Jesus' name.
Blessed Jesus please keep me well in body and
help me to be kind to my family and friends.
O God, I pray to thee Lord be near the elderly people.
Comfort them in body and mind.
Open their hearts to see your love
For them Lord Jesus hear my prayer and answer quickly.
Help our children to follow Thee.
Keep them from drink and drugs and things so bad in life.
Protect them Jesus with your loving care wherever they go.
Lord send your Guardian Angel to watch over and guard our children.
Holy Jesus, child of Mary, glorious Saviour, blessed Lord,
faithful God.
Amen.

Christine Shurey

PRAYER OF A DANCER

Before mine eyes, (before I sleep)
Drift memories; while past echoes meet,
My spirit soars, while I at rest,
Pray for thy help, as I face each test.

I leap to thee - I spin - I skip . . .
And to the ground I bend my knee . . .
Not with my lips, but with my feet
I sing my song of praise to thee!

I press - with strength, I fall - I rise;
I glide, with swan-like majesty . . .
I dart, with speed of lightning's strike -
Then drift again, in harmony . . .

Twisting! Turning! Poising! Still
With all-whirling thoughts my heart doth sing,
Dear Lord, my choreographer -
Direct my steps - control each limb!

Please give me grace, so to perform
With truth and love . . . to bring
Understanding, to all who watch in doubt
And the thought (which is what this is all about)
That *life is this dancing thing!*

Mary McCaig

THE MEDITATORS

Allah, Buddha, Jesus, Vishnu and Gnesh,
the people's Gods and Meditators have
all tried their best,
now its up to everyone to wake up from
their rest.

Put all the things that are so good
about them on display,
and stop the evil in the world from
causing an affray.

Together the good folk could forge a
chain of love so strong,
that no crude bully in the world could
teach them what is wrong.

Our faiths should stand up and complain
when villains use them ill,
lets crawl out from this darkness all
that stops us is the will.

Jean Paisley

EXPERIENCE

From the canyons to the sky
From the ocean to the sea,
From pain to happiness -
You've given me . . .
Experience, so strong
That I've come a long way
I thank you for life -
Which I live every day.

Iris Cone

BEDTIME PRAYER

Dearly beloved
and ever loving Holy Father.
Who sees, hears and understands
all things in Heaven and on Earth.
If it is thy will
through thy infinite spirit
to heal
all those who are sick and suffering
in mind,
in spirit,
and in body,
regardless of race, colour or creed.
Wherever they may be
especially the children,
the homeless
and the animals.
Thy will be done
Amen.

B Bowles

PEACE WITHIN

Loving Jesus come to me,
Fill my heart with love for thee,
From all this anger here within,
When I hear of other's sin.

Lord I cannot bear the sight,
For those who suffer day and night.
No food or shelter, naught they have.
But anguish and the pain.
Keep them safe within your arms,
With all your love remain.

Set them free from all they fear
To a new life full of joy and love so dear.
Dear Lord hear us when we pray
For a perfect peaceful day.

Maud Sales

HEAVENLY BLISS

In the warmness of thy wings
Let's forget all earthly things;
In the glow of things celestial
Let's forgo man's nature bestial.
Tune our minds, Lord, to the heavens,
No more being at sixes and sevens
With fellow men; let's help each other
Avoiding ills and similar bother.

John de Graft-Hayford

I Give Thanks

I give thanks that at the close of day
I have spent it well in industry and play . . .

And hope in doing so, I've done a good deed,
To family, friend, or someone in need.

I give thanks that at the close of day,
I've lived a day worth living, in some small way.

Barbara O'Grady

HOPE IN YOUR HEART

When in times of sorrow,
Or in deep despair,
When the one that you have loved,
Is no longer there,
Then give yourself to Jesus,
And feel the warmth of his pure love,
And someday when God calls you . . .
You will meet in heaven above.

Till then . . . when you feel the sun
Warm upon your face,
And the soft gentle breeze caress your
Cheek
Remember all the wonderful times . . .
Precious memories . . . these are yours to keep.

Face each day anew with courage,
And keep God within your heart,
Live life, to be true and honest,
And of God's heavenly kingdom . . .
Someday . . .
You will be a part.

Erica Gordon

PRAYER AND PEACE

Dear Heavenly Father - I love you so
And although my thoughts you know -
May I be 'in your will' I pray
To follow Jesus every day.

I lift above to you in prayer
All my family for your care.
As not all of them know you -
May they in time become quite new.

To be 'born again' I wish for those
Whose lives are dismal (and it shows).
The strangers passing in the street
Who tread so wearily on their feet.

'Tho as Christians we can have joy -
I pray for comfort for each girl and boy.
So hard to be a child these days
For the world has different ways.

O God above to thee I pray
For your special peace as I lay
In my bed and so to sleep -
Counting blessings instead of sheep.

Pat Melbourn

PRAYER OF LOVE

Dear Lord, I pray that I and others
may find peace and love in our hearts.
Then in unity, dear Lord, I pray
that we can send this peace and love
to those who need it.
To comfort their pain, to soothe them with love.
To caress them with divine light.

I pray that all people may grow together
and progress in your beautiful garden of love
and understanding. Under your absolute guidance.

Amen.

Anita Messer

THE SLEEP FAIRIES

Here come the sleep fairies from the sleepy skies
Caring their sleep dust for your sleepy eyes.
They've come to see the children, all the girls and boys
Sprinkling their sleep dust when there is no noise.
They sit upon your eyelids when you're tucked up safe in bed,
Will only come to see you when this story has been read.
You can sometimes hear their voices when your eyes are shut tight,
They play round on dream clouds in the middle of the night.
They chase away your nightmares and keep the bed bugs out,
They will only come and see you if there's no-one else about.
When you wake they fly away until tomorrow night
For the little fairies do not like daylight.
So go to sleep now children, it's time for them to come,
They're waiting for the kisses from your dad or mum,
So here come the sleep fairies from the sleepy skies,
You can sometimes find their sleep dust in the corners of your eyes.

Daren Peary

LULLABY

The evening is nigh
With darkening sky,
'Tis not now so bright overhead,
Time now, to place baby into her bed,
Freshly bathed and attired,
To lay down its head,
For the night to be retired,
Then to softly croon a soothing tune,
Sleep to inspire, soon after saying our prayer,
The sandman will be there, for he too will you admire!

Benny Howell

YOU ARE THERE

The pillow waits, the bed is warm,
from work and worry we are torn,
it feels so good now to lay down,
and pity those who can't be found,
those in war, those who thirst,
those who suffer here on Earth.
After light the darkness comes
and our fears should be left alone.
To pray and rest and sleep in care
we thank you God, for being there.

Maureen Bell

GIVE ME STRENGTH

This prayer is just a short one,
I don't want to ramble on,
But all I really need, Lord,
Is the strength to carry on.

I need to earn my daily bread,
I have to pay each bill.
I want to help my fellow man;
I simply can't be ill!

I've everything to see to
Now I'm left all by myself,
And it's not that I'm complaining
About being on the shelf;

But I'm just a *little* woman
And my years of youth have gone,
So, in your loving kindness,
Give me strength to carry on!

Jean Oxley

CHILD'S PRAYER

Dear Lord,
When little Jay Morris
Goes to bed at night,
I pray he will sleep soundly,
And wake up feeling bright.
While angels do watch over him,
May all his dreams be good,
May he learn to love his neighbour,
As everybody should.
Amen.

Elaine Sturman

A Prayer For Anyone

Lord, be with those we know overnight,
Make it right
For those we *don't* know until the morning.
Let tomorrow's light
Bring hope to those who are hopeless,
Help to those who are helpless,
And love to those who are loveless.
To those who are lost, and to those
Who search for them,
Give your strength and peace.
Amen.

Jacquie Richardson

A Prayer For Fulfilment

Dear Father, creator of all life.

Help us to feel your divine presence in
All things, knowing you are the provider
Of all our needs; which are given with
Great love.

Teach us to love unconditionally, accepting
Others as they are, without criticism, but
With praise. May we feel your peace within
Us, for until then we cannot live in peace
With others.

Let your light shine forth in all we do,
Drawing those around us into its beam so
They may share the joy it brings.

Help us to see with our spiritual eyes;
Working with our fellow men and all that
Inhabit this planet towards making the heaven
On earth you desire.

Teach us to give freely of ourselves, to love
Unreservedly, and serve wholeheartedly, knowing
Our strength comes from that part of us that
Is you. In this may we find our fulfilment.
Amen.

Carole Fowles

GOD SENT US

Mummy, before I shut my eyes to pray
I would love a cuddle and hope you'll stay.
It is my warmest wish to give my love
As it is you and daddy that brought us from above.
Heaven is where our Lord Father is to be,
And mummy, I was God's choice that we grew in your family tree.
Now I shut my eyes to put my hands together.
I pray that our family will love each other for ever and ever.

Alien 3

POSITIVE

If you go to bed feeling rough
Tired of routine and had enough
Spare a thought for those without a cause
The homeless, the ones involved in wars.

Be thankful you are still alive
Mistakes to rectify you can strive
For you have a tomorrow to make it right
While others will not see out the night.

Not everything is as black as you paint
Be positive, think without restraint
Concentrate on your strengths, be proud
Tell yourself 'You're great' out loud.

N C Bain

THE AGEING NIGHT

The shutters close so gently
Fibres seal the skin,
Thought revolves around your day
Then slumber enters in.
A jolt back to a memory
A twitching aching joint,
Trembles in a weary breast,
You reach the turning point.
The mind, a void of eerie light,
The body limp and still.
No one enters with you and no one ever will.
A lonely path before you
Until the dawn of day.
A puzzle plagued with pictures
That slowly fade away.
Refreshed, with daylight rising
Another world to face.
You made it through the ageing night
With God's Almighty Grace.

Shirley Sammout

CHILD

Tonight . . . I am a child.
I try to be all
That a mother should try to be - what should a mother be?
Am I just endlessly
Shouting
And ordering?
Daily, I'm bordering
On some insanity,
Lord, come and
Mother me . . .
Loved, as I want to be
Held unconditionally,
Rock me and snuggle me . . .
Make me your child
Tonight.

Helen Mary Miller

I Thank You

As my loved ones lie asleep
I close my eyes to pray
For the safety of each and every one of them
As my lips begin to say

I thank you for the life we have,
The life you let us lead
And hope you continue to love us
As I fall fast asleep.

Joleen McPartland

THE BOGEYMAN

As I went up the stairs at night
I'd be as quiet as I can
Because I didn't want to see that
Thing they called the Bogeyman.
He was hiding in the attic and he
Was always sneaking around.
But whether he was up there, he
Never made a sound.
I looked inside my wardrobe and
Searched beneath my bed.
I knew he was lurking around somewhere
And he made me fill with dread.
I'd lay in bed at night and hope to
God and pray.
That he would listen to my prayer
And make him go away.
I'd close my eyes and shut them
Really, really tight.
Too scared to open them in case
I got a fright.
I'd lay there in the darkness
And pull the covers right over my head.
As I heard the floorboards creak
This is what I said,
Dear Jesus, please will you hear me as I pray,
I promise I'll be a good girl tomorrow
If you make him go away.
Then I'd hear the voice of
Jesus as he said don't be afraid
I'm right here by your side.
He made me feel so safe and on
my pillow I cried.

Thank you Jesus, I'm your
Very number one fan.
Because you taught me to believe
That there was no bogeyman.

Carol McCann

A Prayer For Tonight

Thank you for this morning,
Thank you for today,
For keeping my family safe
As they go along life's way.
I pray for all who are in trouble
In lands so far away.
May you watch over and protect them
I ask tonight as I pray.
Amen

S Askew

A Child's Prayer

Now that it is time for bed
'Let's say your prayers' my mother said.
But I want to say one on my own
So I am kneeling here alone.

Today, I've not been very good
I haven't done the things I should
I've argued with my sister small
And drawn with pencil on the wall.
I was sent into my room
For hitting the cat with the garden broom.

Dear father can you tell me please
Why I am naughty with such ease?
Never want to do what's right
I really love to have a fight.

Tomorrow I will change my way
I'll be good (for part of the day)
Then if I've made you sad today
Tomorrow you'll be glad to say
'This one's a friend of mine
He tries so hard (most of the time)'
So Father just as this day ends
Can I please just say *'Amen'*.

Dawn Parsons

Sailing Sleepy Seas

My bed is my yacht to sail into sleep,
I prepare to start on my trails,
Travelling moonlit oceans of deep
As the gentle wind catches my sails.
Nothing is ever quite what it seems,
Mists can soon become clear,
I am the captain of bountiful dreams
Imagination is limitless here.
Tonight I may reach an island of old,
Share feasts with a grand tribal king,
Listen to ancient tales they were told,
Join in with the songs that they sing.
Then when it's time to start on my way,
I'll give thanks to the new friends I've made,
'Hoping to see you again' they will say,
'New stories of magic we'll trade.'
So as I board my ship and head home,
A deep slumber I find myself in,
Tomorrow I'll set off on the waves tipped with foam,
Another adventure will begin.

C MacAlister-Cottrill

MY PRAYER

Bless me, Lord, please hear my prayer.
Bless all at home and families everywhere.
I tried today, but failed, to be as good as yesterday.
Forgive me, Lord, show me the way.
Tomorrow, I shall try again.
Please love me always. Amen.

Pauline Conlon

BE NEAR US LORD

For all the sick folk everywhere
Dear Father keep them in thy care.
God pity those who cannot sleep
Thy quiet vigil o'er them keep
For all the sad and lonely pray
Stay by their side both night and day
For those who fear the hours of night
Show them dear Lord your guiding light
And when your call comes at our end,
Be close, be near, thou constant friend.

J Winwood

Heavenly Tranquillity

As I rest my head tonight,
I reflect upon my thoughts today.
You lay me down to rest in peace,
And comfort me in your special way.

From your throne in heaven above,
You look down and are proud of me.
I know throughout the day gone by,
You were carrying and blessing me.

Your angels guard me through the night,
You keep me under your wing.
Your spirit guides me through my life,
I'll trust you in everything.

If you choose to give me breath tomorrow,
I know you'll still be here with me.
But if you take me to those pearly gates,
I'll stay with you for eternity.

Kelly Hurn

PRAYER FOR THE START OF EACH DAY AND NIGHT

Teach us good Lord
To serve you as you deserve.
To give and not to count the cost
To fight and not to heed the wounds
To toil and not to seek for rest
To labour and not to ask for any reward
Saving that of knowing that we do your will.
Lay down to sleep, I pray the Lord my soul to keep.
If I die before I wake,
I pray the Lord my soul to take.

P Pattel

A 'Curative' Prayer

Dear Subconscious,
Thank you for keeping me alive so far.
I am now going to lie down and relax.
I am going to lie down - and relax.
I am going to relax, until I fall asleep -
Whilst I am asleep, I want my subconscious to
Ensure that my sleep is a deep, restful sleep,
From which I will awake - fully refreshed
Happy and pleased with the world.

Subconscious mind, whilst I am in my deep, restful sleep
It is all right now, for you to repair any ailments I may have.
It is time now to tell any cancerous cells, or other harmful cells,
That it is all right for them to die now, then I can get better, and
I will lead a longer, more healthy, active life.

Robert Hessey

Thoughts Of Mine Own

Dear lord, I do not come unto thee as often as I should,
A long time it has been, yet I come unto thee this day
To give my prayer and thanks
For the true and lovely sweetheart, who is ever by my side,
Who thee, Oh Lord, sent to me.

I wish to thank thee for her heart, full of love,
Which I hold mine sweet one.
Thanks thee dear Lord for mine own.
I too ask of thee to ever keep her well and hers.
May she know every joy and single happiness too.

I too beg of thee, to ever give me the strength
To work hard for her, to help to assist me
To cherish, adore, to love her more. To love her more each day.

Again, dear Lord, I do thank thee for sending me a true love
Who is as beautiful as the flowers on thine earth.
Thanking thee again, dear Lord. Amen.

Denys George Hill

ABBEY DEAR

I look at you with your eyes closed tight
As I kiss your cheek and bless you goodnight
I stand and watch you for a while
And my heart swells up as I give a smile.

Abbey dear, I hope the world treats you well
Do your homework as your father often has to tell
Keep safe and let the world treat you right
As I pray for you each and every night.

We brought you into this world, a blessing to keep
As I see you in your peaceful sleep
No-one to harm you, to cause you pain
For if they did, your father would go insane.

Abbey dear, sleep another night through.
When you awake in the morning remember we love you
And will stand forever by your side
You're our Abbey who gives us so much pride.

Abbey

GRATITUDE

Blessed are the trees
Who give me shade

Blessed are nature's spirits
Living in the glade

Blessed is the breeze
Which cools my blood

Blessed be the sea
In ebb and flood

Blessed be our sun
Giving heat and light

Blessed are all stars
Who come out at night

Blessed be our Earth
For providing us a home

Blessed is my life
For being free to roam.

Deborah Hall

SOULS

What does a soul mean to you.
Is it something on a shoe
Or perhaps a fish on a plate
Or a poor soul at the gate.
To me it means everything
I feel it comes from within
If we listen to it every day
Like our consciences
We won't go astray
Don't sell your soul for luxury
Or the Devil will take it, believe me.

Joan M Tapping

BEDTIME DREAMTIME

Hush my child, lay down your head,
The time for sleep draws near,
Hush my child, lie safe in bed,
No need to fret or fear.

Rest my child, drift off and dream,
Spread your wings with ease,
Rest my child, my bright sunbeam,
Be taken with the breeze.

Fly my child, to distant lands,
With wonders far and wide,
Fly my child, to sea and sands,
Woes ebb upon their tides.

Return my child, from dreamland deep,
With happiness not sorrow,
Return my child, and wake from sleep,
To start afresh the morrow.

Sarah L Scotcher

A New Day Will Dawn

Before we rest and go to sleep,
We ask the Lord for favour.
That he will watch as darkness comes,
As we pray, our faith won't waver.

When shadows fall and evening comes,
Will we look back with sorrow?
Or will we be proud of things achieved
And start anew the morrow.

Dawn comes once more and shadows fly,
Bringing brightness and light again.
The colours are beautiful and pure,
Like the bow just after the rain.

Smoothly it comes, not making a sound.
A new day so glittering bright,
Stretching its fingers out over the ground,
Covering all like a blanket of light.

The gloom of darkness is chased away,
The sun is here for the day.
It brings with it new promise,
Of another chance to play.

Will we make this day worthwhile?
and for others do a good deed.
Helping someone along the way,
Maybe help a family in need.

A new opportunity comes each day,
With the glory of the sunrise.
To start again all bright and new,
This is the way to be wise.

Valerie M Bacon

THE WORLD OF SLEEP

Once again the Journey is upon me and one that I must take as the
World of sleep
beckons to me as the end of day is nigh
No matter what I try to do my eyes now so heavy all I can do is sigh

What a trip this sleep can be, as from this World I seem to shift
but where do I go, where am I, as I start to sleep and drift

I hang as though suspended, safe yet up so very high
another World it must be and yes I feel as though in a mist
a feeling of calm and being so free and I fly through space and time
as though they do not exist

I do not miss that World I left behind that was mine
the day before my night of sleep
that brings me to so many shores and visits I know that I must keep

I want to remember when I awake so many wondrous things
but can I, will I do this
as in the past something is blocking and to my memory clings

I feel I am moving back toward a bright new day somehow near
but also far away
And yes I can see the Night has gone and light is here for me
but I will search for memories until sleep returns for me

John Hooley

LORD HOW LONG?

How long will it take me to die Lord,
Not as long as this life that I live!
How long will the darkness last Lord,
And what sort of light will you give?

Why am I here at all Lord,
What good do I do on this earth,
Is there a part for me Lord?
Please help me to prove my own worth!

I'm getting very tired Lord,
Please help me stay one more day.
Just help me to exist a while longer,
Until all my debts I may pay.

I think I've endured enough Lord,
So now let me go in peace.
I want to be free from the past Lord,
Please let this unhappiness cease!

Maggie Roberts

A Single Rose

New Year's Day, winter all around
New Year's Day, frost on the ground
Another year, another day and not one sound
A flower grows - a single rose.

Some years ago if I recall
Some years ago, not many at all
Darkness was all around and slaughter did abound
But a flower grows - a single rose.

                        A rose of France called Pace
                        And in my garden grew
                        And helped to pull me through
                        A single rose.

Will this mark the start of a thousand years of peace?
Do we start a new, lay to rest the troubled beast?
Can we now hold a brand new feast?
A flower grows - a single rose,
A single rose.

Philip London

A Prayer For Everyone

For everyone who has touched my life
of whom I am aware
I pray the Lord will keep them safe
Supported with his loving care.

For everyone I've yet to meet
of whom I'm unaware
I pray the Lord will keep them safe
Supported with his loving care.

For everyone I'll never meet
there will be many I'm aware
I pray the Lord will keep them safe
Supported with his loving care.

Grace D Frackleton

MY PRAYER

Heavenly Father,

    Help me to be more loving, to all that I meet,
    as I journey through my life.
    May I be ever mindful of the love that you
    show to the world.
    Grant that I may have the optimism to rise
    above all my negative thoughts.
    To see the good in everyone and not to dwell
    on the imperfections and unhappiness in the world.
    For by my love and optimism, I can change the world,
    and make it a better place to live in.

                                        Amen.

J Painting

THE STRIFE OF LIFE?

May God in heaven welcome with open arms,
A mere, humble mortal who has experienced joy and qualms.
Although my life has meandered a rocky course, and I've paid the price,
All I ask of you is, *'Am I worthy of Paradise?'*

John P Evans

THANK YOU

In this troubled world needing love to mend
Lord, you know sometimes it's hard, thank you for being a friend.
You're only a prayer away when my life is troubled
You show me the way, you give me a reason to believe.
Thank you for daylight and the stars at night
Thank you for the changing seasons most of all the spring
Thank you for the blackbirds that sing.
Thank you for every passing storm cloud, every drop of rain.
Thank you for the gift of time, all the love and happiness it can bring
Thank you for our world in which we all play our part
Most of all, thank you, for love which we carry in our heart.
Thank you for our eyes to see
Thank you for those angels at night who watch over me.

K Lake

PARENTAL POETRY

As I hold you
In my arms
And gaze up at
The moon so high
The stars all twinkle
And I start to pray
That, you'll keep safe
For another day.
That I'll do my best
To keep you from harm
To love and protect you
To make you strong
That no matter what
Tomorrow brings
Our hearts will always
Be full of love
And sing.
So, as I rest
Your weary head
And lay you
In your tiny bed
I hope you have
The best of dreams
That give you hope
And joyful things.

Teresa Webb

NOT JUST A BEDTIME PRAYER

'God'
'Can you hear me up their?
I've only got a few minutes on this wet and windy April day,
So listen very carefully, or else I won't talk to you again.'
Why?
Does religion cause such heartbreak and fears?
The TV's full of it and it fills me up with tears.
The terrifying, tearing, tortuous stripping of the soul out of a country.
Why does man destroy a country all in the name of religion?
They may have their differences but they can be overcome by
patience and sensible discussion.

I put some money into Tesco's Aid bucket yesterday.
Every little helps they say, but I feel so helpless.
Looking at my bags of goodies and thinking, they have nothing,
not even pride in their country.
They have no country.
I'd have some in my house tomorrow if I was asked.
I'd go and help with the aid workers if I was asked.

But, for now, keep all that are suffering safe from harm,
With shelter, food and warmth.
They are frightened, running scared. Their faith is lost and they
may even question you.
So, God, listen to me and tell them that I care.

Frances Doe

A Goodnight Kiss

Hush little one.
Hush and go to sleep.
I know you do not want to.
Hush, hush, and do not weep.

Life has been such fun today,
and nothing else you wish to miss.
But God will bless you in the morning;
So, hush, hush, a good night kiss.

Philip Trivett

UNTITLED

Dear Lord I thank you for my health,
Sweet Lord I thank you for my wealth,
The wealth of love my family brings,
Not money, jewels, material things.
Please teach my children how to care,
And know that you are always there,
To ease their pain or any sorrow,
That they may come across tomorrow.
Open their eyes to this wonderful world,
To the beauty of nature around us unfurled.
Bless each of my grandchildren as they sleep
And may all their dreams be happy and sweet,
So when they wake they'll be sure to find,
They are healthy in body as well as mind.

Yvonne Johnson

EVENING PRAYER

Dear Lord
>Before I close my eyes,
>Wilt let me speak with Thee?
>Not as my judge, but as my friend,
>My priest, confessor be?
>
>Thus have I sinned, both great and small,
>Without a show of sorrow,
>As, without doubt, I shall commit the same again tomorrow.
>That I am wicked, weak and vain,
>Cruel, cold and worldly-wise,
>This do I not deny, dear Friend,
>Nor gloss them in Thine eyes.
>But, if You can just understand
>And not in righteous anger from me speed,
>Then will I lay me down to sleep
>In peace, My Lord, indeed.

Sheila St Clair

IT WAS ONE OF THOSE DAYS, LORD!

The Boss was in a foul mood
again;
My Nursery Nurse was ill and did not
arrive;
A boy was sick all over the new
carpet;
Another had a tantrum, loud and
long;
A full pot of bright paint was
spilt;
A much longed for assembly was
cancelled.

But then, Lord ...

The sun began to shine;
A child gave me a cuddle;
Another made me laugh;
Two shared a book quietly;
Some made a model together;
A parent said 'Thank you.'

Lord . . . Tomorrow is another day.
Help me to realise and trust that with the 'rough'
You also send the 'smooth'.

J V Lisle

WHEN YOU SLEEP

When you lay down your head,
To rest your tired eyes,
You sleep upon this pillow,
You dream about the lies.

When your thoughts are taken from you,
To be emptied of hate,
You wander through the sky,
You step upon your fate.

When all your secrets have spoken,
To leave your tired head,
You see them disappear,
In a pool by your bed.

Katie Burt (14)

THANK YOU

Another day,
Near its end
One more message
I'd like to send
To thank you Lord
For giving me
My ears to hear
My eyes to see
My hands to touch
The things I see
Thank you for
Creating me.

Susan Davies

THE PANDA

Pricked with a pin in moments of passion
A ruined hot water bottle and confusion
Water dripping along table and floor
A young boy cried as he ran to the door.

He went to the garden to find flowers
Comfort was needed, he waited for hours
Spoilt was the panda but what could he do
Pray for forgiveness was all that he knew.

The panda now flat lay on the table
Circled with daisies, name on a label
He knew he would miss the warmth of his friend
The animal was dead and would not mend.

Sent upstairs in disgrace, punishment came
His panda was buried, he was to blame.

Evelyn Sharman

A Child's Prayer

Holy Jesus every day,
lead me by Thy precious hand,
So's I keep a steady path
and from you, not stray.

Holy Jesus I do pray
for Your guidance every day,
At my home and at my school,
at my work and play.

Holy Jesus I thank Thee
for Your tender love and care,
And for blessings I receive,
every night and day.

Holy Jesus I do pray
for my family and my friends;
Bless and keep them safe and sound,
where e're they be.

Holy Jesus every night,
Let thy Spirit guard me tight;
Let thine Angels o'er me watch,
whilst I'm fast asleep.

Geo K Phillips

A Bedtime Prayer

I pray God keeps you safe my dear
And you can flourish for another year
I pray he keeps you safe and sound
Like I surely myself have found.

I see you sleep and catch a breath that's true
And I surely know that God has blessed you
Goodnight, God bless, my dear one
Wake up to a new morning sun.

God blessed the coming of your birth
As he blessed the beginning of the earth
He shall continue to carry you through
And watch all the wonders that you do.

God bless, I await you in the morning
Rosy cheeks constantly yawning
I shall feel an inner sense of calm that's true
To know that the dear Lord has blessed you.

Tracey Marie

BLESS YOU ALL

When at night sleep will not come
Just lie quietly and pray for them all
Go back thro' the years, and ask God
To keep them free.
Free from loneliness, free from pain
And tell them to wait, 'cause I'm on my way
To sit there beside you, when it comes my way
Bless my little daughter with eyes so wide and blue
God took her for an angel, after an hour or two
Bless my husband, my lover and friend
A squeeze, a cuddle would help no end
Are they chatting together, talking of the loves they did have
Do those three guys talk together
Of the love that they all shared
Do they realise that I am the one
Who loved them all to despair
Too late, I did realise that only one was true
But 'twas that time, too late for me
Because your life was through
All I can do, dear Lord, is pray
For all three men that I loved so
Bless them all I do say
I really loved them in my way.

Sheila Wall

SONG FOR A FULL MOON

Glorious milky shine!
Glorious silky mine!
My midnight orb of beauty.
Your big bright eye,
keeping watch over me.
Fain that I should
Stop loving you
And fain that you should
Stop shining.

Silk and shine
The eternal insomniac
Guarding my sleepy soul
My glorious milky shine!

Laura Cruickshank

Guidance

O Lord our heavenly Father, I want to thank you
For every thing that has made today happy.
Please forgive me for everything I have done wrong
And stay close by me and those I love,
Through Jesus Christ, Our Lord.
Amen

N Callear

POEM FOR A CHILD

Little one, close your eyes and go to sleep
Dream nice thoughts, all your problems let me keep.
Anything you feel you cannot share
Take it to Dreamland and leave it there.
For in the dawning of a new day
You will find it easier if you have
Unburdened yourself along the way.
Life is full of tests that you will have to face
But all these issues can be dealt with
If you just have a little faith.

Ann Grimwood

THE LAST PRAYER

Lord God, we know we must hear
A prayer so sent so many times
That in the dark of darkest days
The dawn your hand is near

And in dreams now spent
Our hopes are with us yet
A light shines far
Nor can it fade, life to beget.

To some horizons to follow far
Far away. For others it may be
The last prayer that they can pray
Only a dawn their own foresee.

What these do ask
We ask this too
That humans and animals
Know not despair as Thou are true.

John Amsden

PRIVATE CONFERENCE

Distant traffic hums
nocturnal industry moving forward

Cold, milky dregs
chipped mug; the worn, battered table

Flat, threadbare slippers
shuffling on dappled moonlit rug

Tired mattress sags
embracing her sad, crumpled bones

Furrowed lips move
silently surrendering utterances

Countless days have closed for her like this
thanking God.

Jacqueline Lopez

A Cry In The Wilderness

Lord: I stand in the shadow of thy wings
Lift me up, I shall fall along the way
Be thou my mentor, be thou my mentor
Throughout each night and day.

All wisdom speaks and understanding hears
A weight of finest gold will not compare
When fear is brought by folly to ourselves
We know our own despair.

Lord: I stand in the shadow of thy wings
O, Perfect One, The loud Hosanna's cry
Within thy tender care, I pray I'll be
If fault does not deny.

My sins will take flight about the garment
But where are all my sins to hide on me?
Judge me not in anger, Lord Jehovah
I stand in need of Thee.

George Lockwood

THE POLE STAR

Who leadeth me
To this prodigy
Before a window glass
Due north
To bow my head
In sacrament
See a star
Of noble birth.

Irene Gunnion

INTO GOD'S HANDS

O God, Who holds all things in settled place,
Surrounding all our searchings with Your grace,
We come before You at this time of rest
Aware of just how deeply we are blessed
As we pursue our journey in Your sight:
Accord us Your protection for this night.

Forgive our failings and our lack of care;
Help us escape self's dangerous dark snare
And know the weakness we should try to mend:
On Your enabling help we must depend.
In all our frailty You can raise us -
You showed us how to drain a bitter cup.

For gift of home and work and family
And friends and health we thank You constantly:
If some of these should cease to be our lot,
We know You'll see that comfort fails us not.
You will uphold us if our path is hard -
Your struggling servants You'll not disregard.

As we close down our minds for nightly sleep
And sink into that helpful world so deep,
We pray to lie there safely in Your hands,
Watched over by the One Who understands;
Then one day at the proper time, we pray,
Lead us to realms of everlasting day.

Anne Sanderson

CATCH THE SUNSHINE

Heavenly Father thanks for such a
beautiful day, sun shining brightly
with my sister did play. God bless
Mommy, Daddy, Sister Bonnie and me, thank
you Jesus for the lovely jelly we had for
our tea. Dear Jesus my prayers are
sent by angels every night, clasping
my hands together, shutting my
little eyes tight. Dear Jesus we love you
send you our heavenly wish. Catch
the sunshine dear Jesus and I'll
blow you a kiss.

Ann Hathaway

INFORMATION

We hope you have enjoyed reading this book - and that you will continue to enjoy it in the coming years.

If you like reading and writing poetry drop us a line, or give us a call, and we'll send you a free information pack.

Write to :-
**Triumph House Information
Remus House
Coltsfoot Drive
Woodston
Peterborough
PE2 9JX
(01733) 898102**